BEANO® BUILDS

GO-KART

BEANO® BUILDS
GO-KART

HOW THIS BOOK WORKS

Dennis loves causing mischief, whether he's speeding around town on his skateboard or racing on his go-kart with Gnasher. Want to be just like Dennis? Now you can with this amazing book which will show you how to make your very own Beano Go-Kart.

Follow the step-by-step instructions, which will walk you through how to create your own go-kart, racing helmet, racing flag and racecourse. There are JUMBO stickers at the back of the book for you to decorate your cardboard creations with. You'll need some basic craft supplies, some BIG cardboard boxes and LOADS of imagination. You might also need an adult to help you… but that's OK. Your go-kart won't be big enough for them!

Once you've built your go-kart you'll also find some games and puzzles to complete. Name your go-kart with the awesome name generator, solve the go-kart racecourse maze and find a friend to race in the Beanotown Go-Kart Race game.

WITH THIS BOOK YOU CAN MAKE...

AN EPIC GO-KART

BEANO 1

PAGES 6-15

A RACING HELMET

PAGES 16-19

A RACING FLAG

PAGES 20-21

A RACECOURSE

PAGES 22-25

PLUS... GO-KART-THEMED ACTIVITIES AND GAMES TO COMPLETE!

GO-KART DIY

Your go-kart is going to be the fastest, awesome-est, Beano-est go-kart the cardboard world has ever seen. You could even make more than one and race your friends.

You'll need a few supplies and a friendly adult to help you cut, glue and measure. Once you've made your go-kart, it's best to keep it somewhere dry (it is made of cardboard after all!), but it's a great toy to play with both inside and outside.

Follow the step-by-step instructions and get an adult to do all the tricky bits, so you can save your energy for running around in your new go-kart!

MAKE SURE YOUR CARDBOARD BOX IS BIG ENOUGH FOR YOU TO SIT INSIDE!

YOU'LL NEED:

✔ A large cardboard box

✔ Scrap pieces of cardboard

✔ A ruler or tape measure

✔ A craft knife or scissors (to be used by a grown-up only!)

✔ 1.5 metres of webbing or rope

✔ 1 metre of rope

✔ Strong glue (or a glue gun - to be used by an adult only!)

✔ High-tack masking tape

✔ A pencil

✔ Paints, colouring pencils and craft paper

✔ An adult to help you cut, measure and glue

STEP 3

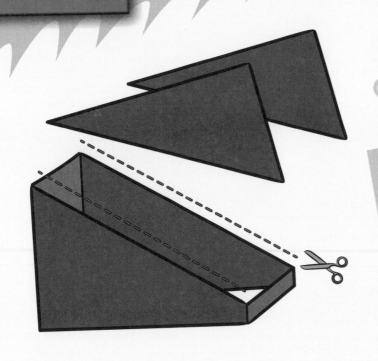

ASK AN ADULT TO CUT THE TWO SIDE PANELS, FROM THE TOP LEFT CORNER TO THE BOTTOM RIGHT CORNER, KEEPING THE 5 CENTIMETRE STRIP ATTACHED AT THE BOTTOM.

STEP 4

FIND THE FRONT SECTION THAT YOU REMOVED IN STEP 2 AND GLUE OR TAPE IT TO THE FRONT OF YOUR GO-KART SO THAT IT STICKS OUT IN FRONT. OVERLAP THE PANEL UNDERNEATH THE GO-KART TO MAKE THE JOIN STRONGER.

STEP 5

x4

FIND THE FOUR WHEEL STICKERS AND STICK THESE TO THE FLAPS THAT YOU REMOVED IN STEP 1. ASK AN ADULT TO CUT THE CARDBOARD TO THE SIZE OF THE WHEELS AND THEN MARK A HALFWAY POINT ON THE BACK OF EACH WHEEL.

STEP 6

GLUE TWO WHEELS TO THE SIDES OF THE GO-KART AS SHOWN, CAREFULLY MATCHING THE HALFWAY MARK TO THE BASE OF THE BOX. LEAVE TO DRY.

SPREAD GLUE ONTO THE TOP HALF OF THE BACK OF EACH WHEEL AND PRESS ON TO YOUR GO-KART.

STEP 7

GLUE THE LAST TWO WHEELS TO THE FRONT SIDES OF THE GO-KART. MATCH THE HALFWAY MARK TO THE UNDERNEATH OF THE FRONT SIDE PANEL AND LEAVE TO DRY. YOU MIGHT NEED TO STRENGTHEN THIS WITH SOME TAPE.

STEP 8

ASK AN ADULT TO CUT A HALF OVAL FROM A PIECE OF CARDBOARD TO MAKE THE BACKREST AND ATTACH TO THE REAR OF THE GO-KART. MAKE SURE THIS IS THE SAME WIDTH AS THE BACK OF YOUR GO-KART.

STEP 9

x2

TO MAKE THE SPOILER FOR THE BACK OF THE GO-KART, ASK AN ADULT TO CUT TWO RECTANGLES THE SAME HEIGHT AS THE BACKREST WITH A WIDTH OF 10 CENTIMETRES.

STEP 10

GLUE THE TWO RECTANGLES TO THE BACK OF THE GO-KART AT AN UPWARD ANGLE, ATTACHING THEM TO THE SIDE PANELS. STRENGTHEN WITH TAPE IF NEEDED.

ASK AN ADULT TO HELP YOU IF YOU GET STUCK DOING THE MATHS FOR STEP 9!

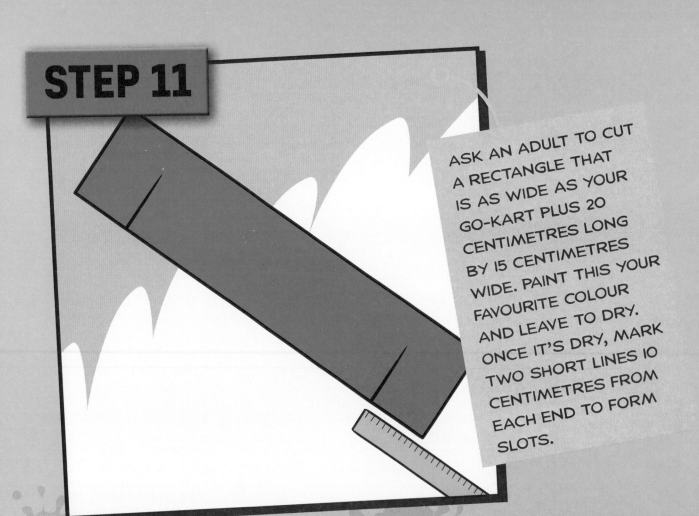

ASK AN ADULT TO CUT A RECTANGLE THAT IS AS WIDE AS YOUR GO-KART PLUS 20 CENTIMETRES LONG BY 15 CENTIMETRES WIDE. PAINT THIS YOUR FAVOURITE COLOUR AND LEAVE TO DRY. ONCE IT'S DRY, MARK TWO SHORT LINES 10 CENTIMETRES FROM EACH END TO FORM SLOTS.

STEP 12

ASK AN ADULT TO CUT THE LINES YOU MARKED AS SLOTS AND FIT THEM ON TO THE SPOILER BARS FACING AWAY FROM THE BACKREST. YOU COULD ADD GLUE OR TAPE TO MAKE SURE THIS STAYS IN PLACE.

STEP 13

IF YOU WANT TO RUN AROUND IN YOUR GO-KART, ASK AN ADULT TO ATTACH SOME SHOULDER STRAPS BY LOOPING SOME WEBBING OR ROPE THROUGH HOLES MADE IN EACH SIDE OF THE KART.

STEP 14

TO MAKE THE STEERING ROPE, ASK AN ADULT TO CUT A LENGTH OF ROPE. MAKE TWO HOLES AT THE FRONT OF THE GO-KART, ONE NEXT TO EACH WHEEL. LOOP THE ROPE THROUGH THE HOLES AND TIE A KNOT AT EACH END.

STEP 15

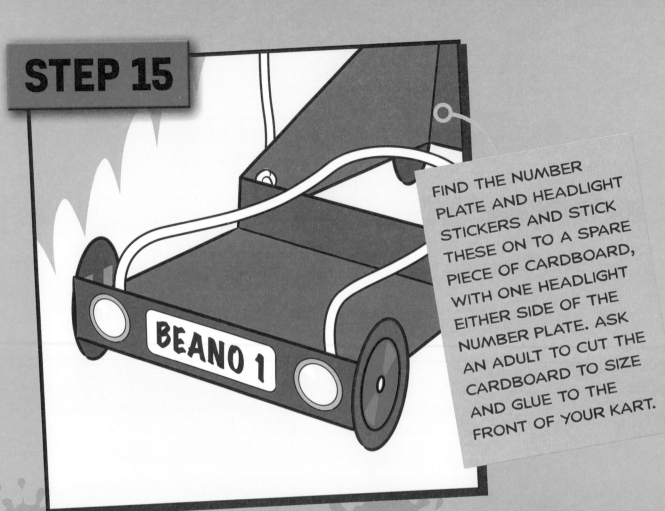

FIND THE NUMBER PLATE AND HEADLIGHT STICKERS AND STICK THESE ON TO A SPARE PIECE OF CARDBOARD, WITH ONE HEADLIGHT EITHER SIDE OF THE NUMBER PLATE. ASK AN ADULT TO CUT THE CARDBOARD TO SIZE AND GLUE TO THE FRONT OF YOUR KART.

STEP 16

ADD ANY OTHER STICKERS OR DECORATIONS YOU WISH, TO MAKE THE GO-KART YOUR OWN! TURN TO PAGE 30 TO FIND OUT THE NAME OF YOUR GO-KART - WHY NOT PAINT THIS ON THE SIDE?

STEP 17

BEANO 1

WOW! YOUR GO-KART LOOKS FANTASTIC. IT MIGHT EVEN BE COOLER THAN DENNIS AND GNASHER'S GO-KART. TURN TO THE NEXT PAGE FOR AN AWESOME RACING HELMET DIY PROJECT.

RACING HELMET DIY

Dennis and his friends might be mischief-makers, but they know the importance of wearing a helmet. This awesome DIY project will show you how to make your very own racing driver helmet.

You can't use this helmet on your real bicycle or skateboard (because it's made out of newspaper and glue, and that won't protect your noggin), but you can use it when playing in your cardboard go-kart.

Follow the step-by-step instructions. You'll need an adult to help you with the cutting and to make sure all surfaces are protected – this one gets a bit messy!

THIS DIY PROJECT TAKES A BIT OF TIME BECAUSE YOU GNEED TO LET EACH LAYER DRY.

YOU'LL NEED:

✔ A medium-size balloon

✔ An old newspaper, or scrap copy paper, torn into strips

✔ PVA glue

✔ Water

✔ A mixing bowl

✔ A paintbrush

✔ A craft knife or scissors (to be used by a grown-up only!)

✔ Paints

✔ Something to protect the work surface and your clothes

✔ An adult to help you cut, measure and glue

✔ A small bucket or bowl

STEP 1

BLOW UP A BALLOON. MAKE SURE THAT IT'S BLOWN UP SO IT'S BIGGER THAN YOUR HEAD, SO THE HELMET WILL FIT! PLACE THE BALLOON IN A SMALL BUCKET OR BOWL SO IT STANDS UPRIGHT.

STEP 2

CREATE A PAPER MACHE MIXTURE (3/4 PVA GLUE TO 1/4 WATER) IN A MIXING BOWL. USING THE PAPER MACHE MIXTURE, ADD STRIPS OF NEWSPAPER TO THE BALLOON USING A PAINTBRUSH, LEAVING THE BOTTOM OF THE BALLOON CLEAR. CREATE THREE LAYERS. YOU'LL NEED TO LET EACH LAYER DRY FOR FOUR HOURS.

MAKE SURE YOU PROTECT CLOTHES AND WORK SURFACES!

STEP 3

POP THE BALLOON AND REMOVE IT. ASK AN ADULT TO TRIM THE BOTTOM OF THE HELMET FLAT, SO YOU CAN FIT YOUR HEAD INSIDE, AND TO CUT A VISOR HOLE.

STEP 4

PAINT THE HELMET IN YOUR FAVOURITE COLOUR AND LEAVE TO DRY. IF YOU USED NEWSPAPER YOU MIGHT NEED TO ADD A LAYER OF WHITE PAINT FIRST SO THE PRINT DOESN'T SHOW THROUGH!

ONCE THE PAINT IS DRY, ADD SOME STICKERS TO PERSONALISE YOUR HELMET AND MAKE IT LOOK EPIC. NOW YOU'RE READY TO RACE IN YOUR GO-KART!

GO-FASTER STRIPES MAKE IT LOOK LIKE YOU'RE GOING FASTER!

RACING-FLAG DIY

If you've ever watched go-kart racing on the telly, you'll know that there's always someone there to wave a chequered flag at the end of the race.

This DIY project is really, really easy. You could probably do it quicker than the time it takes Dennis to disappear after a prank goes wrong.

Follow the step-by-step instructions to make your own racing flag!

IF YOU CAN'T FIND A DOWEL OR A CHOPSTICK, YOU COULD EVEN USE A GNICE STRAIGHT STICK. BUT GNOT ONE FROM MY STASH.

YOU'LL NEED:

✔ A wooden dowel, measuring roughly 0.5 x 20 centimetres (or an old chopstick!)

STEP 1

FIND THE RACING FLAG STICKER IN THE BACK OF THIS BOOK AND CAREFULLY PEEL IT OFF. PLACE IT IN FRONT OF YOU STICKY-SIDE UP.

STEP 2

PLACE THE WOODEN DOWEL IN THE CENTRE OF THE STICKER, SO THE TOP OF THE DOWEL IS AT THE TOP OF THE STICKER, WITH A HANDLE STICKING OUT AT THE BOTTOM.

STEP 3

FOLD THE STICKER IN HALF, ENCLOSING THE DOWEL. CAREFULLY LINE UP THE EDGES OF THE STICKER AND PUSH OUT ANY AIR BUBBLES. YOUR FLAG IS READY TO WAVE! ON YOUR MARKS...

RACECOURSE DIY

A go-kart would be no fun if you couldn't race in it, so why not make your very own obstacle racecourse?

Find some friends to compete with, then set out your obstacle racecourse to see who is the fastest go-kart racer in Beanotown.

Follow the step-by-step instructions and then ask an adult to help you lay out the course in a garden or open space.

SAVE EVERY BOX YOU CAN FIND TO ADD TO YOUR OBSTACLE COURSE.

YOU'LL NEED:

- ✔ Empty boxes of various sizes
- ✔ High-tack masking tape or artist's tape
- ✔ Paints, colouring pencils and craft paper
- ✔ Lengths of rope to mark out the course
- ✔ A garden or a big open space you can set your course up in
- ✔ An adult to help you cut, measure and glue

STEP 1

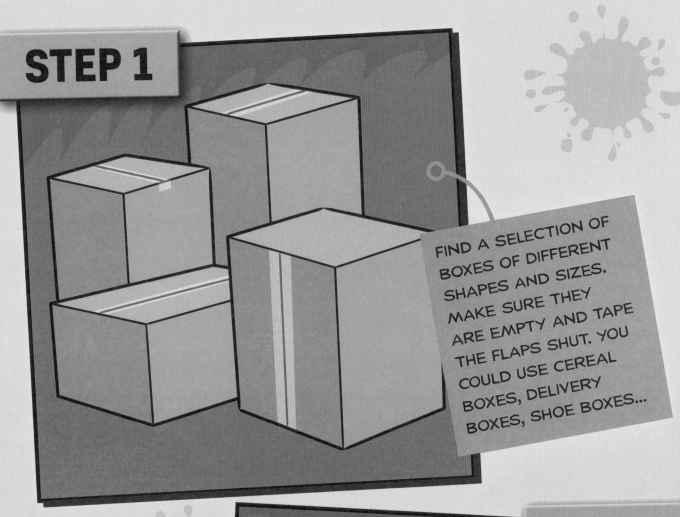

FIND A SELECTION OF BOXES OF DIFFERENT SHAPES AND SIZES. MAKE SURE THEY ARE EMPTY AND TAPE THE FLAPS SHUT. YOU COULD USE CEREAL BOXES, DELIVERY BOXES, SHOE BOXES...

STEP 2

DECORATE THE BOXES USING PAINTS, CRAFT PAPER AND STICKERS. YOU COULD EVEN MAKE THEM LOOK LIKE BUILDINGS FROM BEANOTOWN! ONCE DECORATED, LEAVE THE BOXES TO DRY.

STEP 3

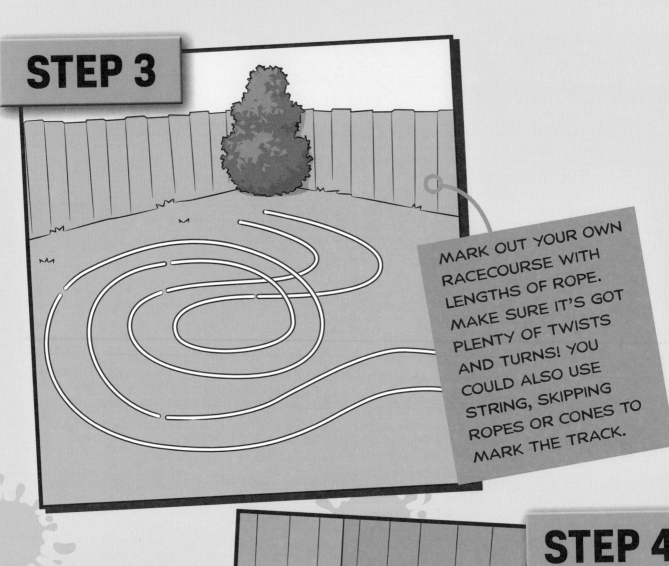

MARK OUT YOUR OWN RACECOURSE WITH LENGTHS OF ROPE. MAKE SURE IT'S GOT PLENTY OF TWISTS AND TURNS! YOU COULD ALSO USE STRING, SKIPPING ROPES OR CONES TO MARK THE TRACK.

STEP 4

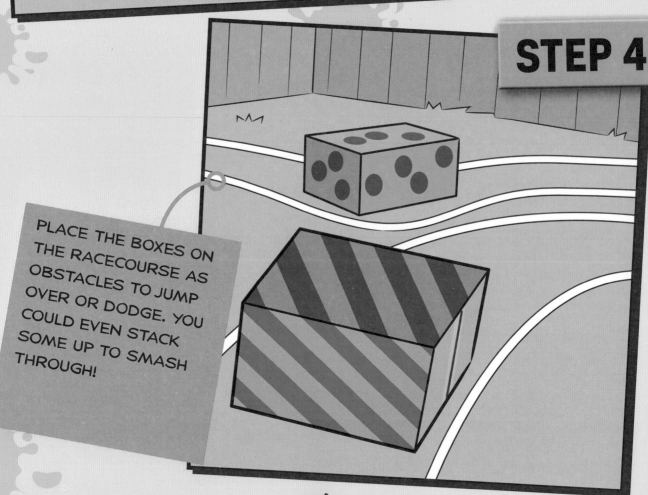

PLACE THE BOXES ON THE RACECOURSE AS OBSTACLES TO JUMP OVER OR DODGE. YOU COULD EVEN STACK SOME UP TO SMASH THROUGH!

STEP 5

ASK A GROWN-UP TO HELP YOU MARK OUT YOUR COURSE.

FIND SOME FRIENDS TO RACE AND SEE WHO IS THE FASTEST. FOR AN EXTRA TRICKY CHALLENGE, YOU COULD RUN WHILST WEARING YOUR GO-KART!

THE BEANOTOWN GO-KART RACE

It's the annual Beanotown Go-Kart Race. Choose whether you want to race as Minnie or Dennis, and see who's going to take the trophy home!

YOU'LL NEED:

- ✔ Two players
- ✔ A dice
- ✔ Counters

WHAT TO DO:

1. Find the counters on the sticker sheet and stick them to a piece of card. Ask an adult to cut them out for you.

2. Roll the dice – whoever rolls highest goes first.

3. Take it in turns to roll the dice and move your counter round the board, following the instructions on the squares.

4. The first one to reach the finish line wins!

DISASTROUS DIRECTIONS

Dennis is trying to direct his remote-controlled car around this maze. Follow the instructions and see if you can reach the finish, and then design your own maze on the next page.

Directions

1. Turn left and go forwards 2 spaces
2. Turn right and go forwards 2 spaces
3. Turn right and go forwards 1 space
4. Turn left and go forwards 2 spaces
5. Turn left and go forwards 4 spaces
6. Turn right and go forwards 2 spaces
7. Turn right and go forwards 3 spaces
8. Turn left and go forwards 2 spaces
9. Turn right and go forwards 1 space
10. Turn left and go forwards 1 space

FINISH

VERY HEAVY WEIGHT INDEED

DANGER!

START

MENACE MAZE

Design your own maze in the grid below, using drawings and the obstacle stickers from the sticker sheets. Then write instructions on how to get from the start to the finish.

Ask an adult to help you set up your maze in real life using anything you can find as obstacles. Climb in your go-kart and then ask someone to read your instructions out. Did you manage to get out of your own Menace Maze?

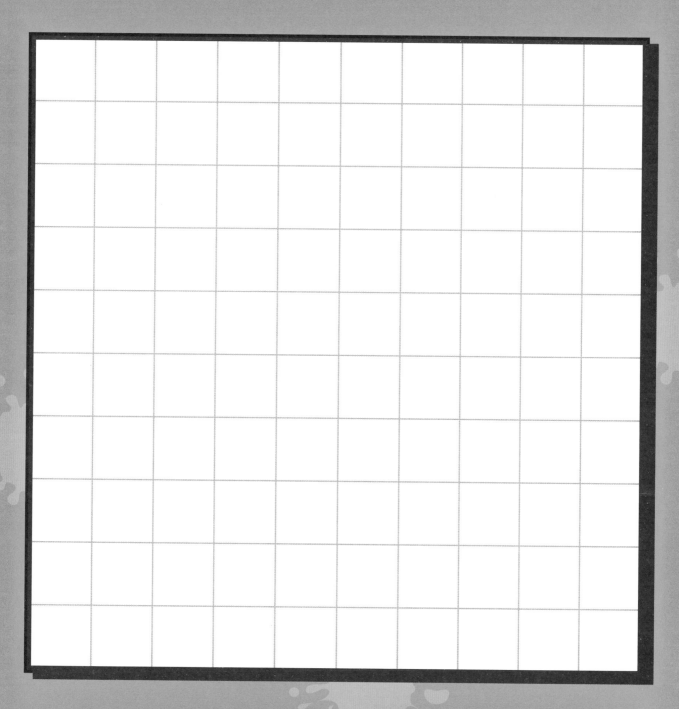

NAME YOUR GO-KART

Your go-kart needs a Beano-rific name, and you can find the perfect one for your new set of wheels below. Simply use the first letter of your first name and your birthday month to name your go-kart!

Find the first word of your Go-Kart's name by using the first letter of your first name:

A - Speed	J - Nimble	S - Flying
B - Doom	K - Plodding	T - Enduring
C - Catastrophe	L - Unlikely	U - Gnashing
D - Parp	M - Amazing	V - Crafty
E - Fuzzy	N - Silly	W - Whirlwind
F - Sneaky	O - Zippy	X - Awful
G - Glittery	P - Terrible	Y - Brilliant
H - Stinky	Q - Mischievous	Z - Fabulous
I - Awesome	R - Spectacular	

Find the second word by using the month you were born in:

January:	Ninja	July:	Kart
February:	Mobile	August:	Monster
March:	Rocket	September:	Goliath
April:	Monkey	October:	Whizz
May:	Prankster	November:	Snail
June:	Menace	December:	Parp

My go-kart is called The _____ _____

WORD SEARCH RACE

Every go-kart racer needs to know the mechanics of their go-kart.
See how quickly you can zoom through the words in this word search.
To make it more interesting, time yourself.

```
H  B  F  O  M  W  T  M  T  K  P  K  C  H  H
D  E  T  O  U  R  H  S  O  S  J  Z  O  Y  N
L  U  T  S  A  E  P  E  S  O  E  V  U  C  R
J  E  G  K  M  E  R  W  E  O  Z  T  R  T  R
Q  K  O  E  E  P  M  D  F  L  F  Z  S  V  V
L  G  H  D  O  E  A  R  V  Z  S  W  E  A  N
J  O  E  B  W  W  Z  U  M  Y  E  Y  A  Q  F
L  H  T  I  Q  B  M  F  J  K  M  N  R  Q  E
K  L  H  S  Q  K  W  A  U  V  P  G  Z  Q  K
H  U  W  H  J  S  V  J  O  D  O  U  X  V  R
H  K  R  P  T  P  P  P  L  T  T  O  R  O  K
E  N  I  L  H  S  I  N  I  F  S  V  M  Q  B
S  P  C  G  I  J  K  A  M  T  T  V  H  D  O
E  W  T  B  G  K  B  J  T  W  I  G  R  M  W
E  C  A  R  A  J  R  S  F  K  P  R  N  Q  D
```

GO KART	FASTEST	WHEELS	PIT STOP
RACE	FINISH LINE	COURSE	
SPEED	DETOUR	ZOOM	Time Taken:_____

31

ANSWERS

DISASTROUS DIRECTIONS

WORD SEARCH RACE

```
H B F O M W T M T K P K C H H
D E T O U R H S O S J Z O Y N
L U T S A E P E S O E V U R R
J E G K M E R W E O Z T R R R
Q K O E E P M D F L F Z S V V
L G H D O E A R V Z S W E A N
J O E B W W Z U M Y E Y A Q F
L H T I Q B M F J K M N R Q E
K L H S Q K W A U V P G Z G K
H U W H J S V J O D O U X M R
H K R P T P P P L T T O R O K
E N I L H S I N I F S T V M Q B
S P C G I J K A M T T V H D O
E W T B G K B J T W I G R M W
E C A R A J R S F K P R N Q D
```

GNEED A HINT? ASK SOMEONE ELSE TO GIVE YOU A CLUE BY LOOKING AT THE ANSWER PAGE!

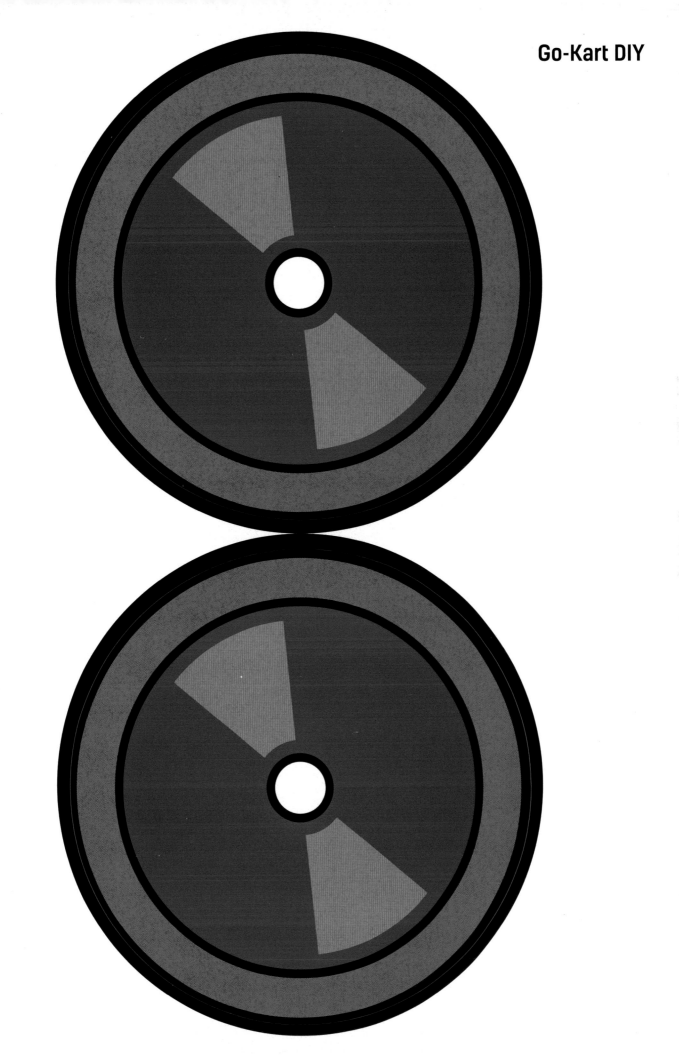

Go-Kart DIY

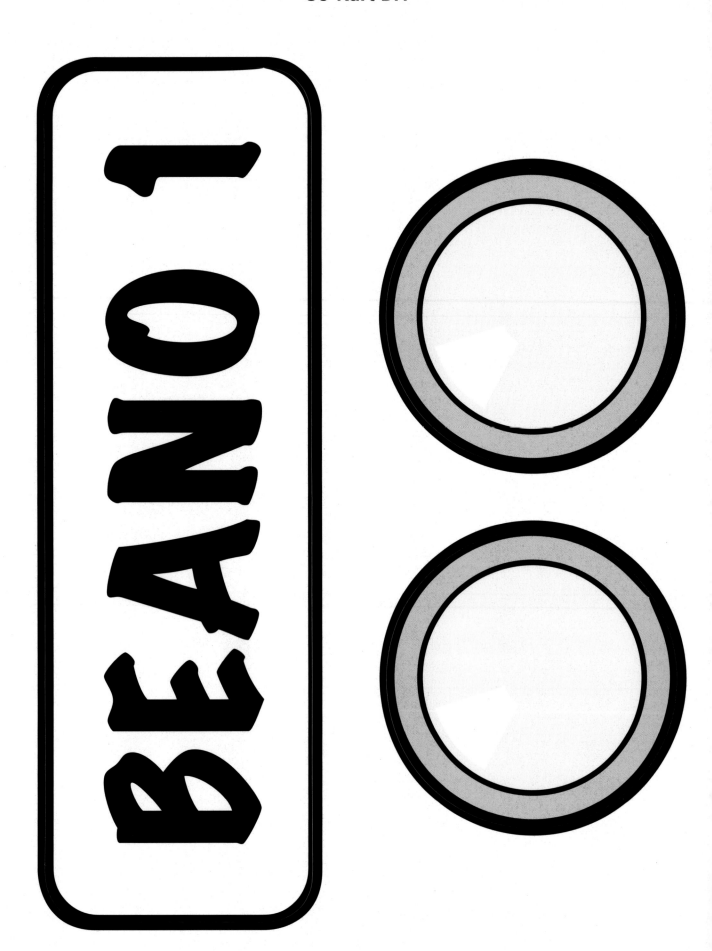

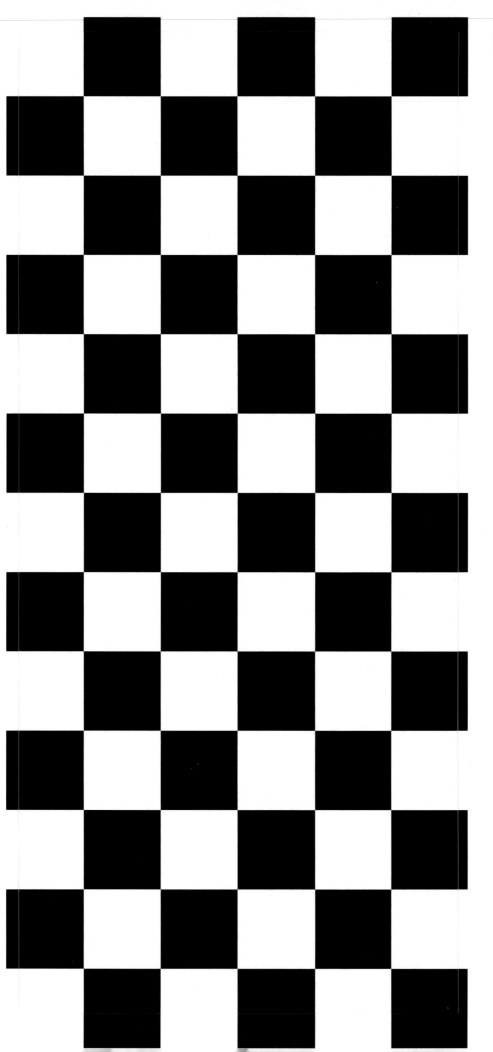

Racing Flag DIY

Go-Kart DIY

Menace Maze

Beanotown Kart Race Counters

Just for Fun

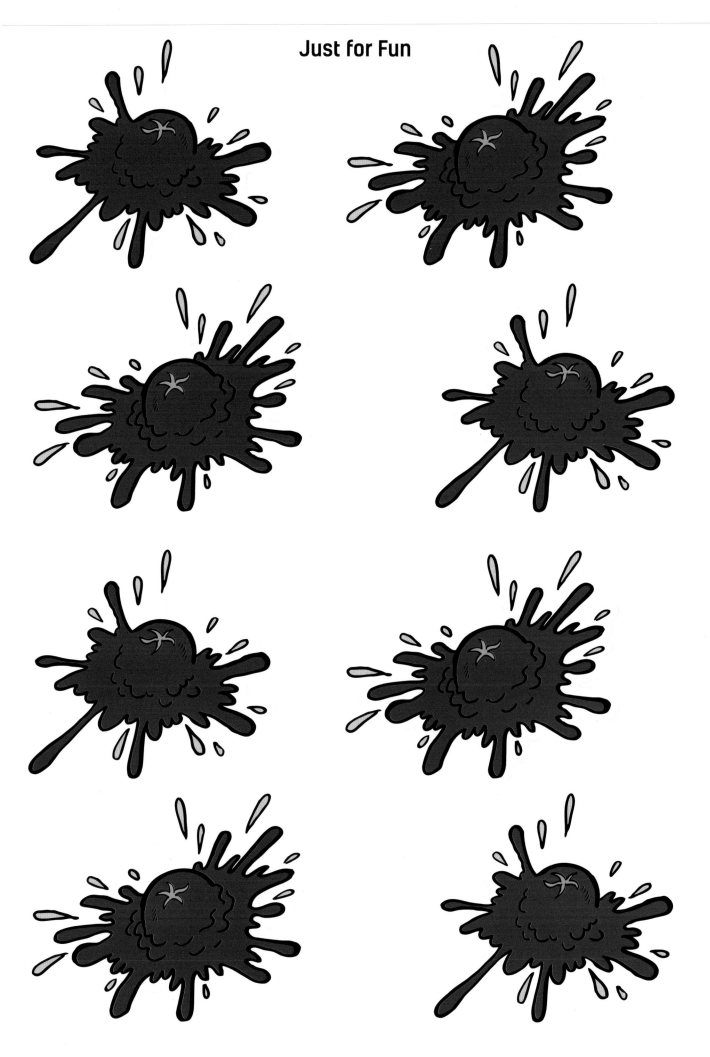

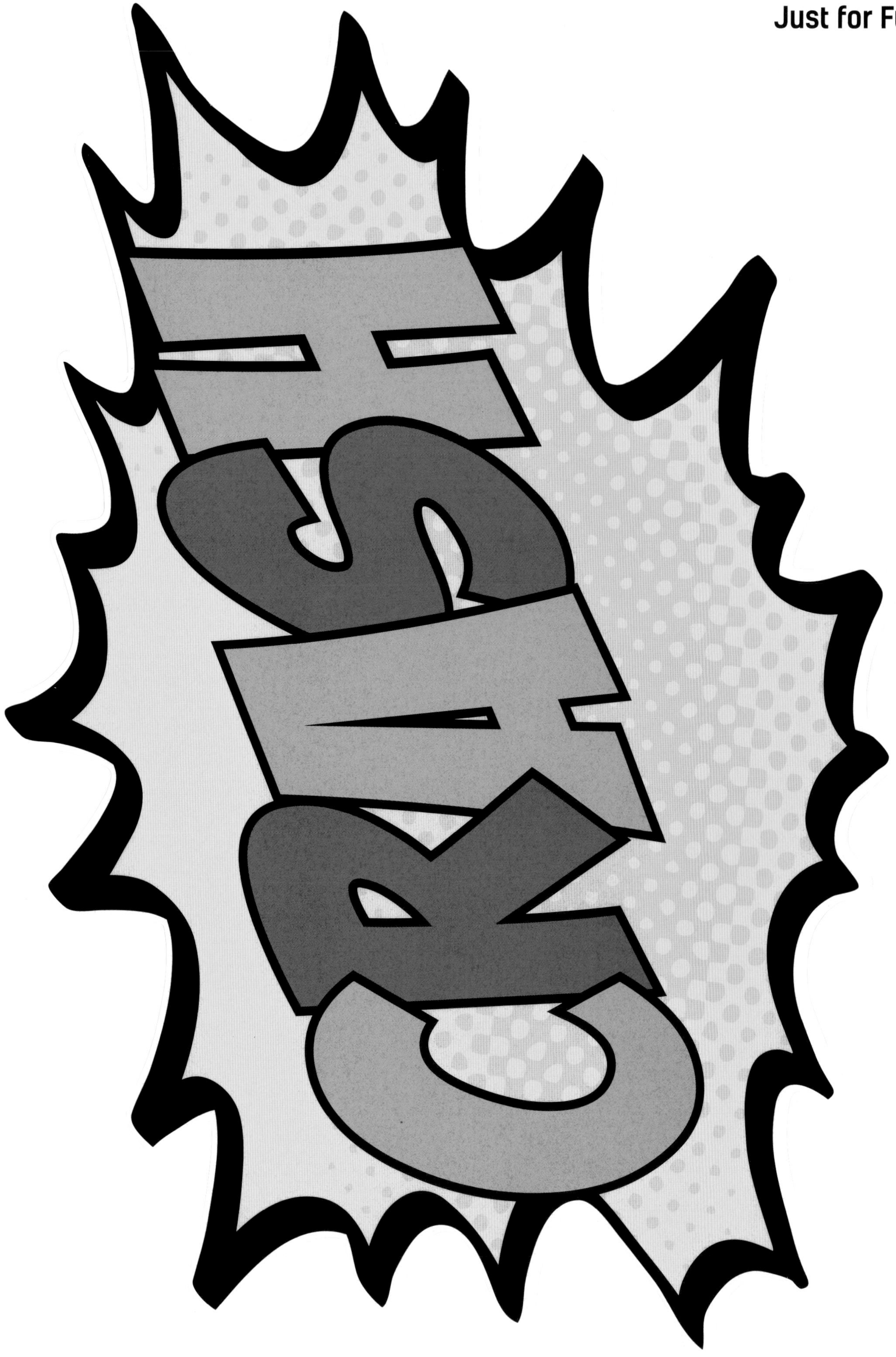
CRASH

Just for Fun